A Time to Talk and a Time to Listen

A Time to Talk
and
A Time to Listen

A Practical Guide to Communication in the Home

Tinuola M. Agbabiaka

iUniverse, Inc.
Bloomington

A Time to Talk and a Time to Listen
A Practical Guide to Communication in the Home

iUniverse books may be ordered through booksellers or by contacting:

iUniverse
1663 Liberty Drive
Bloomington, IN 47403
www.iuniverse.com
1-800-Authors (1-800-288-4677)

ISBN: 978-1-4759-0516-8 (sc)
ISBN: 978-1-4759-0518-2 (hc)
ISBN: 978-1-4759-0517-5 (e)

Printed in the United States of America

iUniverse rev. date: 03/29/2012

DEDICATION

To my soul mate – Oriyomi; whose
unreserved, undying love and support
means everything to me.

ACKNOWLEDGEMENTS

TO GOD BE ALL THE GLORY

CONTENTS

INTRODUCTION

"Communication is a skill that you can learn. It's like riding a bicycle or typing. If you're willing to work at it, you can rapidly improve the quality of every part of your life". Brian Tracy

C ommunication is the number one important thing in any relationship and the lack of it is also unarguably the major challenge that exists among people in the society. In modern society, communication has been seriously eroded, there is now such a constant barrage of information from different sources such as the television, mobile phones, texts, personal computers and mobile hand-held devices that makes communication in the home almost impossible.

All this intrusion from external sources has caused major disconnects within families and in relationships and has invariably led to misunderstanding what the other party in the home or in a relationship is saying. It is the inability to understand the other person that causes misunderstanding and creates strife between two people.

Communication must be received for it to be effective. Very often, women lament bitterly on how they could no longer understand their spouses and the men also fall into this dilemma.

1

For communication to exist between two people, they must both be willing to work at it.

It is usually one party that closes the communication lines which often leads to frustration for the other if repeated attempts to reopen communication lines are rebuffed.

The first step, however, is to understand what communication is and the different ways one is able to communicate; next is to understand each other's language. If I speak German, for instance, and the person I need to communicate with neither speaks nor understands German, communication with words cannot take place. I will need to use other forms to pass across my message.

Everyone has a preferred way of communication. Therefore, it is important to learn the way the person we desire to communicate with communicates. This will definitely help in connecting with the person and passing across the message.

According to Dr. Gary Coleman in his book, *The Five Love Languages*, he narrowed the different ways of communicating love to one's spouse down to five languages. Therefore, the main task for every couple is to study each other and learn the most convenient and appropriate language for each other. Individuals are born differently and react to situations differently. While some people may not necessarily mind loud voices, there are individuals who automatically turn off if they perceive that voices are being raised.

As a marriage counsellor, the prevalent issue in most marriages I have counselled is the lack of or misconceived communication. This and many more communication issues have prompted me to write this book. As you read on, you will learn how to communicate with your spouse, children, relatives, in-laws, friends etc. These issues transcend tribe, culture or race. They affect everyone, but hopefully after reading this book you will be able to connect better.

CHAPTER ONE

WHAT IS COMMUNICATION?

"The biggest mistake is believing there is one right way to listen, to talk, to have a conversation -- or a relationship". - Deborah Tannen

Communication is simply put, an exchange between two people. It is a lot more than speaking or hearing. It must be given and received for it to be complete. There are various forms of communication; however the key thing is that communication must be given and accepted for it to be effective.

While many of us feel communication is all about spoken words, statistics show it constitutes only about 7% of communicating. A look, glance or gesture, which constitutes body language, also communicates. Sometimes, words are not necessary. The rest consists of facial expression, tone of voice, body language, perception etc.

Communication can either be deliberate or not deliberate. It differs from culture to culture. What means one thing in one culture may mean something else in another culture.

Everyone has the ability to communicate in one form or the other. Communication is not limited to speech alone. We use a lot of our body parts to communicate. We can communicate with our mouth, hands, eyes, body language etc. There are basically two types of communication –spoken and unspoken. Communication must be constantly present in a relationship for it to survive. It is the only way of keeping up with each other as part of a family or team. As individuals, we change daily as those we interact with also do. Words that we hear and those places that we go influence and change our attitude and perception towards life. Therefore, communication between couples is essential to ensure that the two parties are on the same page, growing together and are not living separate lives.

VERBAL – SPOKEN WORDS
"By words we learn thoughts, and by thoughts we learn life."- Jean Baptiste Girard

Spoken words constitute verbal communication. It involves speech and is vast. In every long-term relationship, verbal communication must be present in order not to be frustrated. Even in inter-racial and inter-tribal relationships, there must be a common language for both parties to converse in to ensure the survival of the union. Every country has its own language with various tribes and religions that also have their local language and/or dialect. Therefore, verbal communication must necessarily include the understanding of the language spoken by any two individuals.

Words must be spoken to the receiver for the communication process to start. Firstly, the speaker must have a clear understanding of the language in order to effectively use it to communicate his/her thoughts while the recipient must understand the words being spoken. For example, if all the sweet words are spoken to me in French and I do not understand a word of French, it would mean nothing to me.

4

- **POWER OF WORDS**

  "Death and life are in the power of the tongue, and those who love it will eat its fruits". Proverbs 18:21 NASB

  Words that proceed out of our mouths are very powerful. They can bring either life or death. Be careful what you say to others and especially what you say to yourself. Negative words eventually translate to negative actions while positive words become positive actions.

  According to ancient history, a Greek philosopher asked his servant to provide the best dish possible. The servant prepared a dish of tongue, saying, *"It is the best of all dishes, because with it we may bless and communicate happiness, dispel sorrow, remove despair, cheer the faint hearted, inspire the discouraged, and say a hundred other things to uplift mankind."* Later the philosopher asked his servant to provide the worst dish of which he could think. A dish of tongue appeared on the table. The servant said, *"It is the worst, because with it we may curse and break human hearts; destroy reputations; promote discord and strife; set families, communities, and nations at war with each other."* He was a wise servant.

- **EDIBLE WORDS**

  "Be careful of the words you say, keep them short and sweet. You never know, from day to day, which ones you'll have to eat."- Anonymous

  Yes, words can be eaten! When we eat words according to the idiom, we take them back and/or admit we were wrong with our statement. We must be careful about the words we speak. It is better to be a man/woman of little words than to be a talkative. When we talk too much, we are prone to not being able to carefully choose our words.

5

Words can also bear fruits, therefore whichever we deem fit to give to someone else; we will surely eat of its fruit. If you speak life with your words, you will definitely eat its fruit. Also, if you speak death, you will eat the fruits. We must be careful of the words that proceed out of our mouths.

- **BENEFICIAL WORDS**
"Do not let any unwholesome talk come out of your mouths, but only what is helpful for building others up according to their needs, that it may benefit those who listen." Ephesians 4:29 NASB
Words that are not beneficial to anyone should not be spoken. We must think and process our thoughts before letting it out. Words spoken must necessarily be of benefit to either the speaker or the listener. Before voicing out thoughts, it is important to check if it is of any benefit.

- **CARELESS WORDS**
"Bu I tell you that every careless word that people speak, they shall give an accounting for it in the day of judgement" Matthew 12:36 NASB
How often do we speak before thinking? We should take time out to process our thoughts with the following checklist:

> *Am I using the right words?*
> *Am I directing the words to the right person?*
> *What do I hope to achieve by using these words?*
> *Will it add value to the recipient?*
> *Must I speak these words?*

Processing the above checklist quickly will most likely serve as a check for us to refrain from speaking carelessly.

Indeed, it is important that we choose our words carefully and ensure the words that proceed out of our mouths have been carefully processed, as we will surely give account for them.

- **HURTFUL WORDS**
  "Finally, brethren, whatsoever things are true, whatsoever things are honest, whatsoever things [are] just, whatsoever things are pure, whatsoever things are lovely, whatsoever things are of good report; if there be any virtue, and if there be any praise, think on these things". Philippians 4:8 KJV
  Words that come out of our mouths are first processed in the mind. The thoughts of your heart will often proceed out of the mouth. Sometimes, this happens in moments of anger or extreme frustration. At times, we blurt out words unknowingly and they are what we were actually thinking. In order not to say the wrong words, we must ensure that our thoughts are clean and try as much as possible to think good of all. *"Out of the abundance of the heart the mouth speaks"* -Luke 6:45.

NON-VERBAL – UNSPOKEN WORDS
"The most important thing in communication is to hear what isn't being said." - Peter F. Drucker

It is often said that non-verbal communication can be more powerful than verbal as it, most times, overrides verbal communication.

- **TONE OF VOICE**
  The tone used in speaking is very important. Your tone may say more than the words you speak and/or pass on more

than you intend to. It is so powerful that when there is a conflict between your tone and your words, and a struggle for supremacy, your tone usually supersedes as the recipient would be more affected by your tone rather than the actual words used. A harsh tone will not pass on lovely messages to the recipient no matter how many nice words are used. On the other hand too, a soft tone will not help delivery in a situation whereby the aim is to show anger. The tone of voice must match the words in order to achieve effective communication. We must remember therefore that in speaking, what we say may not be as important as how we say it.

WHAT CONSTITUTES TONE OF VOICE?

Quality of voice – This is made up of pitch, volume, and style of speaking and delivery mode.

a) **Expression** – The way words are expressed also influences the tone. Expressions must be commensurate with the words used and must match to effectively convey the right message. Harsh and loud words will most probably illustrate anger and displeasure while soft, murmuring, soothing tones can express pleasure or bliss. A high pitch tone may illustrate excitement. A tone that rises in pitch at the end of a sentence indicates a question, whilst one that is nasal and choppy can express irritation.

b) **Perception** – The tone of voice of an individual helps strongly in determining the way he/she will be perceived by other people. A strong, bold, clear and concise tone is perceived as confident and bold while people who speak slowly or at a low volume may be considered weak, timid and/or afraid.

- **BODY LANGUAGE**

  In communicating with one another, your body movements while speaking must be in rhythm. They must be powerful enough to add strength to your message rather than take away from it. For example, walking away, blocking of ears, rolling of the eyes or arms akimbo, all indicate lack of interest in the words being spoken.

  On the other hand, a smiling face, a hug or an embrace are all welcoming; an indication of friendliness and warmth.

- **FACIAL EXPRESSION**

  Facial expressions are an indication and a reflection of what is going on in an individual's mind. Do what you say and your facial expressions match? It is very difficult to mask one's feelings on the face but careful examination will almost always give away the true feelings. For example, a cold stare and/or a non-smiling face or a frown will indicate disapproval or displeasure; so also a smile expresses acceptance and friendliness while laughter expresses joy. Raised eyebrows show surprise and a furrowed forehead conveys fear and anxiety. We must be conscious while communicating to ensure that the facial expressions are correct indications of the message being passed across or received.

TWO-WAY PROCESS

Communication is a two-way process. It must be given and received in the proper context before we can assume a complete process. Often times, the major challenge is in the fact that communication given and the one received may not be the same. The intentions of the giver might not be accurately delivered due to either faulty or tainted delivery process, or the recipient has misinterpreted the message.

LISTENING

"Everyone should be quick to listen, slow to speak and slow to become angry for man's anger does not bring about the righteous life that God desires. Therefore, get rid of all moral filth and the evil that is so prevalent and humbly accept the word planted in you, which can save you. Do not merely listen to the word and so deceive yourselves. Do what it says. Anyone who listens to the word but does not do what it says is like a man who looks at his face in a mirror and after looking at himself, goes away and immediately forgets what he looks like. But the man who looks intently into the perfect law that gives freedom, and continues to do this, not forgetting what he has heard, but doing it —he will be blessed in what he does. If anyone considers himself religious and yet does not keep a tight rein on his tongue, he deceives himself and his religion is worthless." James 1:19-26 NIV

God gave us only one tongue but two ears which is a pointer to the fact that we should listen more than we talk. A big part of communication is listening. The freedictionary.com defines listening as *"to make an effort to hear something"* or *"to pay attention: heed"*. The importance of listening in communication is huge and for communication to be said to be complete, there must be listening. While the ability to speak well is a necessary ingredient for good communication, so is the ability to listen. Most people tend to focus more on their speaking ability and sometimes go on self-improvement workshops on speech; however, working on listening should equally be taken seriously.

One easy way we can work on our listening skills is to practise with those around us – our spouses, children, friends and colleagues.

Once we are done with a conversation with them, we can try to recap and see how well we have listened. We should come to the understanding that it is when we listen that we learn. We learn about the person speaking and about what he/she is trying to say.

Listening and hearing are two different things and shouldn't be confused with one another. Listening is a deliberate act, while hearing is the act of perceiving sound. Listening requires active effort. When you listen, you are able to hear what is being said and also some things not said. In other to be able to listen effectively, we must do the following:

- **Pay attention:** In order to listen to someone else effectively, we must not be distracted. We need to pay attention to the speaker. Doing other things while trying to listen will mar the listening process. Try and keep your attention on the speaker. You may take out distractions like switching off the television, radio, computer, laptop, phone etc. If possible; you may separate yourself and the speaker to a secluded area if the environment is noisy and distracting. Concentration is the key ingredient. Concentrate on the speaker and do not allow your mind to wander off. There is the tendency to begin to daydream or think of other things if we lose concentration.

- **No interruptions:** Keep quiet. Allow the speaker to have his/her say. You gain more by listening, as you will be able to retrieve information about the speaker. Do not cut short other's conversation. Apart from the fact that it is rude to interrupt, it is also an indication that you are not listening. You must be patient enough to allow the other person to convey his/her thoughts. Even in situations where it takes some few seconds for the speaker to convey his/her thoughts

11

into words, a good listener will wait through till the other person finishes before speaking.

- **Do not make assumptions:** Making assumptions while listening is a sure way to stop paying attention. By assumptions, you would have arrived at what *you* believe the speaker is trying to convey and that is detrimental to effective listening. The truth is that you may be wrong as to the message the speaker is trying to convey. Our assumptions are sometimes based on perceptions and/or misconceptions about the speaker.

- **Clarification and Verification:** In order to have a clear understanding of what is being heard, the listener may ask the speaker for more clarification. You might hear statements like *"Correct me if I am wrong, but what I believe you are saying is..."*

BODY PARTS THAT COMMUNICATE

- **EYES**
  It is possible to communicate with another person with your eyes. Eyes speak volumes and sometimes the level of closeness with another person may tell the person something about you by just looking into your eyes. For instance:
  a. Red eyes: fatigue, crying
  b. Wink: admiration, approval
  c. Rapid blinking: attention grabber, lying, something in the eyes
  d. Dullness: weakness, illness

- **MOUTH**
  There are various ways to use the mouth to communicate:
  a. Kiss: desire; approval; show of love
  b. Hiss: disapproval; disgust
  c. Whistle: call attention; admire

- **HANDS**
  Our hands can be used in many different ways to get across to the other person:
  a. Clap: approval; appreciation
  b. Touch: show of love
  c. Hold: show of togetherness; unity
  d. Hit: display of anger
  e. Embrace: show of happiness; welcoming

- **HEAD**
  With your head, you are able to pass on the following information:
  Nod: approval; acknowledgement; affirmation; denial; yes/no

VARIOUS TYPES OF COMMUNICATION ISSUES IN THE HOME:

Wives:

- *"My husband talks a lot and barely allows me to mumble a word."*
- *"My husband ignores me completely and does not listen to anything I say."*
- *"My husband walks away during conversation."*

- *"My husband is verbally abusive."*
- *"My husband is a talkative in public but clams up at home."*
- *"My husband is never available to talk to."*
- *"My husband is always too tired to talk."*
- *"My husband ignores the children."*
- *"My husband takes a decision with his relatives rather than me."*
- *"My husband listens only to his mother."*
- *"My husband is afraid to tell his relatives to back off."*
- *"My husband tells his mother and siblings everything that goes on in the house."*

Husbands

- *"My wife talks too much."*
- *"My wife never listens to me."*
- *"My wife ignores me."*
- *"My wife doesn't understand me."*
- *"My wife listens to the advice of friends and relatives."*
- *"My wife is a nag."*
- *"My wife is influenced by her mother."*
- *"My wife is verbally abusive."*
- *"My wife disrespects my mother and siblings."*
- *"My wife disobeys me."*
- *"My wife takes decisions without deferring to me."*

CHAPTER TWO

IN THE HOME

"Feelings of worth can flourish only in an atmosphere where individual differences are appreciated, mistakes are tolerated, communication is open, and rules are flexible - the kind of atmosphere that is found in a nurturing family." -Virginia Satir

Communication in the home is very essential. It is the key to a good relationship in the home. The importance of communication is so great that a lack of it can indeed break a home. The coming together of a man and a woman is for the sole purpose of becoming one and growing together. They share a vision and work progressively towards it. This in effect will create a perfect atmosphere for the raising of children. Therefore, if the couple is not communicating, then there cannot definitely be an understanding of the vision. The word of God says, *"My people perish for lack of vision"*.

Imagine a situation where you have no idea of your spouse's goals and aspirations, and neither do you understand your children's thoughts, hopes and aspirations. In such an environment, each individual will do their own thing independently and as a result, work against each other. Such a family will definitely not grow and there will be a high risk of breeding irresponsible children.

ESTABLISHING GROUND RULES

It is often said that where there are no laws, there is no sin. In any home/family, there must be laid down rules. There should be clear rules and guidelines in the home and they must be communicated to all members of the home. Where there are no rules, there is a tendency for chaos to reign and this is detrimental to the survival of the home.

Where there are no rules, anarchy and chaos dwell. Every home must have a set of rules and/or code of conduct that govern the home. It is important to know and understand the origin of the rules in the homes as these rules will be the code of conduct and the basis for resolving issues as they arise in the home. Are these rules based on the word of God or on tradition? When there is a conflict of the two, the word of God must necessarily prevail.

While there are some fundamentals that are better addressed before marriage, it is almost impossible to touch on every area, as a lot of circumstances and situations will present itself during the course of the union. This is when it is very important to rely on the word of God. To avoid misinterpretation, you may approach a faith based marriage counsellor for clarification.

As a marriage counsellor, I can say a good percentage of relationship issues are communication related. It is either one party feels it's unnecessary to share information or the other misinterprets it. Let me tell you about a couple:

Paul and Jane are newlyweds (not their real names). They met while in the university, courted for about six years and had looked forward to the day they would finally be joined in holy matrimony. They were very happy to be finally pronounced husband and wife and looked forward to the beginning of the rest of their lives together.

Having spent such a long time together in courtship, they were pretty sure they knew and understood each other well.

Paul was raised in a polygamous home. His father had three wives and his mother was the second wife, while Jane was raised in a monogamous home with her parents being devout Christians. The difference in their backgrounds was not considered an issue for them as they were of the view that everyone has their own life to live and that was how their parents chose to live theirs.

Once they had decided it was time to tie the knot, they notified their church that insisted that they must undergo counselling classes, which they felt was a waste of their time. After all, they have known each other for six good years! What else could they discover about each other?

Grudgingly, they attended counselling classes, as the church would not join them if they did not attend the classes. However, they missed quite a few classes citing work pressure and traffic jams as excuses.

At the end of the twelve weeks counselling course, they were signed off as ready for the wedding despite attending in reality only about eight of the classes.

Theirs was a big wedding with the venue filled with family, friends and well-wishers. It was the happiest day of their lives. Surely, it was the first day of a lifetime of bliss.

With all the festivities over, they settled down to building a home. In the course of determining financial responsibilities, Paul insisted that he would only be responsible for the house rent and all other financial responsibilities in the home would be borne by his wife, Jane. She was shocked! What kind of man would feed off his wife?

Jane made attempts to reason with him and have them sit and talk through it. They had married as Christians and had the word of God as reference point but Paul would have none of it. She began to see a new side of Paul that she hadn't seen before. She thought she knew him.

By the time she realised she was getting nowhere with him, she decided to seek counsel as she knew they needed help. This couldn't be happening just two months into their married life. The marriage was becoming a nightmare.

Luckily, Paul agreed to go with her for counselling and he was asked his rationale for believing he was only responsible for the house rent. What was his reason? His father only paid the rent when he was growing up and his three wives had responsibility for everything else which included his father and every child borne by each wife; therefore he does not see any reason the arrangement should change now that he had his own home.

On the other hand, Jane who was brought up in a Christian monogamous home had a totally different view, as her father was the breadwinner while the mother supported in the little way she could. They were devout Christians and believed the word of God.

All attempts to let the man understand his role in the home as the "bread-winner" failed, as the first major fight unfortunately was the last. The couple separated barely six months into marriage!

There should be clear understanding of the roles of a man and his wife in the home. These roles must be communicated *before* marriage in order to avoid major disagreements. The word of God says, *"If anyone does not provide for his relatives, and especially for his immediate family, he has denied the faith and is worse than an unbeliever"* 1 Timothy 5:8 NIV. Whereas with regards to the woman, the Lord said, *"it is not good for the man to be alone. I will make him a helper suitable for him"* Genesis 2:18. NIV

In the case of Paul and Jane above, despite that they have spent so many years in courtship; they failed to communicate with one another their expectations regarding the roles and responsibilities in the home. There are fundamental issues that need to be discussed before a couple can be joined in matrimony. While it may indeed not be possible to anticipate and address every issue before marriage, most of them will have been covered. The importance of this is what has been laid down according to the word of God and God's plan for each home. However, we sometimes have situations where the man will not be able to function as the breadwinner by either of the following reasons:

- Redundancy: the man being laid off
- Higher earner: the wife earns more
- Inability to secure a job

In such a situation, care must be taken to communicate the right message to the children and/or extended family. The right message therefore is what the word of God says.

As seen in the story above, Paul has chosen tradition above the word of God. When that happens, there can only be strife.

AGREEMENT
"Can two walk together except they be agreed?" Amos 3:3 KJV

The principal parties of the home are the couple and it is very important for couples to agree on any issue that affects the home. Naturally, it is clear that as individuals they may have individual fears, views and suggestions concerning issues. However, they must both put aside their individual preferences and reach a compromise for the sake of the home.

When two people are in agreement, they communicate better. They are relaxed with each other and listen more attentively. All these make interpretation very easy and communication will have taken place.

For a couple coming together to start a family, they are embarking on a journey, a journey of life. This is a journey they must take together and there must be a common goal in order to reach their destination. Obviously, agreeing on destination is very important otherwise both parties may end up at different destinations.

DISCLOSURE

It is one thing to reach an agreement with your spouse; it is another thing to disclose it to your family and friends. Sometimes due to sentiments, we tend to allow some of our friends and family members some excesses, which may invariably upset our partner.

If you have agreed with your spouse concerning certain issues, it is only proper and prudent for you to keep to it. The downside is that you run the risk of being paid back in your own coin, which you may not find funny at all. While disclosing your agreed points with regards to your friends and family, you should try and observe the following:

- **Be polite**- there is no point or gain in being rude. While these rules are what govern your home, you must realise that your family and friends have homes too. Respect is reciprocal, so politely pass across your message. While they may not necessarily like or accept what you tell them, they will respect your wishes.

20

- **Be cautious and wise**- There are some information that will have to be passed on to your in-laws by your spouse and vice versa. It bothers on foolishness to go ahead and inform your in-laws of some rules that limit their access into their son or daughter's home.

- **Stand your ground**- Irrespective of how your family and friends receive your set boundaries; stand on it. Do not be fazed by their comments or how unhappy they are about your decision. The most important thing is that you and your spouse have both agreed and will see it through.

CHAPTER THREE

WITH YOUR SPOUSE

"A gentle answer turns away wrath, but a harsh word stirs up anger." Proverbs 15:1 NASB

This is the secret to a lasting marriage: Couples, who communicate effectively, will triumph over any obstacle in the home!

It is indeed not an easy task to communicate with one's spouse as both of you, coming from two different backgrounds, will indeed also have different views, approach and outlook towards life. There are also the different ideas and ways in handling conflicts. These differences are what actually translate into strife if there is no communication.

While communication is important, we must also remember that the goal of effective, lasting and sustaining communication is to have an understanding of your spouse's thought process as well as finding solutions to issues that arise in your relationship.

The goal is not to win! If you seek to "win" an argument or insist on being "right" every time, you will never be able to communicate effectively with your spouse.

Let us consider the case of John and Grace (not real names).

They have been married for about eight years. However, only the first few years were the times they could remember being happy together. They are presently not enjoying the marriage but have chosen to stay in the marriage for the sake of their children.

Their problems began about five years into the marriage when John lost his job and was no longer able to be the breadwinner of the family.

The effect of this is that Grace became the sole breadwinner. Due to pressure of work, home, and the children, she became very irritable and would get angry at the slightest notice. She was bursting under pressure from home and work, but was unable to communicate with John how she felt. She also was of the opinion that John could do more to support her at home and with the children since she was effectively the breadwinner of the home.

John, on the other hand, would have none of this as he was determined to remain the head of the home in every aspect, so would rather spend his time searching for a job. He was not comfortable with having his wife be the "bread-winner" and wanted at all cost to get back to his God given role.

He could not understand the reason he had to lift a finger to support his wife-Grace as she was still his wife anyway and he expects her to fulfil her wifely roles irrespective of the fact that she was the sole breadwinner. He was also getting tired of the now so frequent outbursts from her as he could not understand the reason for the mood swings.

Grace now sees her husband's attitude as mean and strongly believes he is no longer the man she met and fell in love with. Surely, he couldn't have been this mean and she chose to spend the rest of her life with him. Having gotten into several fights with him, she is fed up with the marriage and is very unhappy.

John also is fed up with the marriage. They can no longer have a conversation without it degenerating into a fight. He feels he has lost his manhood.

He is convinced Grace is disrespectful and mean, because she is the one who holds the purse in the household. She wasn't like this when he decided to ask her to be his life partner. They no longer speak except when necessary and only in monosyllables. He believes they would be happier apart.

We can obviously identify the following communication gap from the life of John and Grace above:

a. There wasn't open communication between them, which became obvious when John lost his job.

b. John and Grace failed to have a conversation concerning John's new "status" and the effect it will likely have in the home.

c. Grace did not communicate with John; her feelings of being overburdened and pressurised, in a clear and non-combatant manner, to her husband.

d. Grace did not communicate with John; her expectations of him with regards to areas he could support her in the home.

e. John should also have communicated his fear of losing his "*manhood*" and his desire to get back to his role in providing for his home.

f. Grace has come to the conclusion that John is a mean man.

g. John has also arrived at his own conclusion that Grace was disrespectful because she is the "*bread-winner*".

h. Both John and Grace have failed to seek counsel or help from trained counsellors.

i. They are now only co-habiting in an environment not right to bring up children.

There is a common saying that *"it is not what we say that matters but how we say it"*. It is important in every relationship to learn the *"how"*.

COMMUNICATING YOUR UNDERSTANDING OF LOVE AND THE WAY YOU WANT TO BE LOVED

How very often do we feel we know how to love our spouse and we very well often get it wrong! Most couples get into marriages assuming that the relationship that existed between the couple before marriage will carry on into the marriage to ensure that it lasts forever.

Truth is that, it is rarely so. Most people have a pre-conceived and/or pre-influenced understanding of how their marriage should be and would quickly fall into the role once married irrespective of how they were during dating and courtship (truth is that we all put up our best behaviour during the pre-marriage days).

When this transition occurs, the other party is so shocked that he/she believes that the spouse has changed drastically. These are the times that I often hear statements like *"He was not like this when we were dating, otherwise I wouldn't have married him"* or *"She seemed so sweet during our dating period, but obviously she tricked me into marrying her"*.

If the truth should be told, while there might truly have been deception on either side, this could easily have been identified before marriage if the parties involved had bothered to look closer; there would have been signs howbeit little. Through effective communication, it would have been detected if a prospective spouse gets angry easily or is capable of being abusive. It is therefore very important to cultivate a close, consistent form of communication with your spouse before tying the knot. If for any reason, you are involved or dating someone who doesn't talk much or talk to you, you might consider the trait one of those to note and decide if you will be okay spending the rest of your life with someone who doesn't talk to you.

That is for those who are yet to marry. If you are married and need to communicate with your spouse, and you are asking, *"How can I communicate with my spouse"*? You should try the following:

- **Attention:** Give your full concentration to avoid distractions. Ensure that there is no noise in the background. Put the newspaper down and/or switch off the television. Trying to listen while you are doing something else will not work and will distract your attention.

- **Do not interrupt:** Interruptions during a conversation does not give the speaker the chance to say what he/she wants to say. It will also give the impression that you do not want to listen or are on the defensive. A spouse who wants to talk really wants to resolve issues. You must be willing to listen until your spouse has finished speaking. That's when you will fully grasp the message he/she is trying to convey.

- **Privacy:** Try to be alone with your spouse when you wish to communicate important issues. Having the children, friends or relatives around will indeed limit communication as you will either not be able to say all you wish to convey in their presence or your spouse will feel uncomfortable with their presence and will not listen. Embarrassment may also rob you of the chance to communicate, as your spouse may be too embarrassed to listen. You may also not get the desired response or solution to your words as your spouse may feel compelled to respond in a certain way because of the people present. If you wish to have a meaningful conversation, you must pursue privacy.

- **Choice of words:** Do not use words like *"you"*, *"you never"*, *"you always"*. Try to use a lot of *"I"*'s; *"I feel"*, *"I will like"*, *"I wish"*, *"I want"* etc. Using the words *"you"*, puts the listener on the defensive and he/she will no longer be listening to what you are saying. *"You"* sounds accusatory and if you want your spouse to see things from your point of view, refrain from using *"you"* and your spouse will feel less attacked and be willing to listen to you.

- **Speak the truth:** *"The Lord detests lying lips, but He delights in men who are truthful."* Proverbs 12:22 NIV
  You should endeavour at all times to speak the truth to one another. It does not help your communication lines if you either lie or exaggerate. Saying your spouse has done what he/she has not or using words like *"a million times"*, *"always"*, *"never"*, *"umpteenth time"* to convey derogatory words will discourage your spouse and shut communication lines.

- **Speak life:** *"Death and life are in the power of the tongue; and they that love it shall eat the fruit thereof"*. Proverbs 18:21 KJV
  Watch the words you speak to your spouse. They must be words that speak life and not death. What you say can emotionally kill your spouse. You must be able to communicate without putting each other down or speaking words that will make

your spouse ashamed and lose confidence. The following words must be avoided at all cost:

a. *"I wish I hadn't married you."*
b. *"This marriage is a mistake."*
c. *"I don't love you anymore."*
d. *"I hate you. You are useless."*
e. *"Why can't you be a proper wife/husband?"*
f. *"I should have married my ex."*
g. *"What did I do to deserve a terrible person like you?"*
h. *"This marriage will not last."*
i. *"You are a lousy lover."*
j. *"You are ugly."*
k. *"I can't introduce you to my friends."*
l. *"I will slap you!"*
m. *"You are a terrible mother/father."*

In place of above, the following words should be used:

a. *"I love you."*
b. *"I am proud of you."*
c. *"I'm glad you are mine."*
d. *"I'm glad I married you."*
e. *"You are a wonderful lover."*
f. *"I could not have wished for anyone better than you."*
g. *"You make me happy."*
h. *"You are beautiful in every single way."*
i. *"Thank God for you."*
j. *"I must be the envy of every married man/woman."*
k. *"You are the best thing that happened to me."*
l. *"You are the best gift God gave me."*
m. *"Our marriage will work."*

- **Seek Clarification:** If you are unsure or unclear about what your spouse has said, ask for clarification. Communication is not an easy task and we sometimes find it difficult to convey our thoughts in the right way and manner, therefore, it is very important to seek clarification. Your spouse may have difficulty in getting across to you. You may clarify by asking:
    a. *"Is this what I think you are saying?"*
    b. *"I will like to understand you better, is ....what you mean?"*
    c. *"I do not want to make assumptions, so can you say............ in another way?"*

- **Do not jump to conclusions:** Never jump to conclusions concerning your spouse. Often times, we already have made our assumptions either of the speaker or what he/she has to say. It is better to listen to what your spouse is saying and have an understanding of your spouse's thought process.

- **Be open-minded:** Do not be rigid. Try to see your spouse's point of view. You may not necessarily agree with the point of view, but listening attentively and asking appropriate questions will help keep communication lines open. Do not dismiss or discountenance your spouse's opinions or point of view. Words that show open mindedness include:
    a. *"I see your point of view."*
    b. *"I understand your perspective."*
    c. *"I think your school of thought is..."*

Do avoid dismissive statements like:
    a. *"You never have anything intelligent to say."*
    b. *"I am not interested in anything you have to say."*
    c. *"Those are foolish thoughts."*

d. *"How can anyone think that way?"*

e. *"You are being ridiculous."*

f. *"You are nuts."*

g. *"You must be crazy."*

- **Control your temper:** Do not get upset or agitated if you wish to communicate effectively. You must determine not to get angry. Anger closes communication lines quickly. To reach a logical conclusion, you must put a hold on your temper. You have to understand that anger solves nothing. In actual fact, it worsens the situation. More often than not, when anger sets in, the real issues will be buried and the words said during our angry outbursts will now be the bone of contention, which invariably results in unresolved issues.

  When we are angry, we also tend to say all sorts of things we do not really mean. We are hurting and will lash out at the person we perceive to be the cause of our hurt. Controlling your temper is easy once you determine before the conversation starts not to get angry. Admittedly, it takes two to tango. Even if your partner gets angry, you must not. The following words are usually words used during an angry outburst, which may lead to the end of such conversation.

  a. *"You are not making any sense at all."*

  b. *"Why don't you check yourself before complaining about others?"*

  c. *"You are the cause of everything not working."*

  d. *"How dare you talk to me like that?"*

  e. *"You are wasting my time."*

  f. *"I am very busy you know."*

  g. *"Don't ever call me again for a conversation like this."*

  h. *"That's it. I am done with you."*

i.   *"This conversation is over."*

j.   *"I am too angry for words."*

k.   *"I am out of here."*

l.   *"Who are you to talk to me like that?"*

- **Watch your tone and level of voice:**
  "The quiet words of the wise are more to be heeded than the shouts of a ruler of fools." Ecclesiastes 9:17 NIV
  While trying to communicate with your spouse, you must ensure that your voice should not be raised. Do not shout or raise your voice, as your spouse may feel threatened and/ or hurt. Your tone adds weight to your words. Whatever information you are trying to convey will either be aided or marred by your tone. You must be watchful and careful of your tone.

  The level of voice is also very important. If it is too low and your spouse needs to strain to hear, he/she may lose interest and just allow you to go on without hearing anything. Also, if it is too high, it may be deemed as shouting. You must speak clearly without any attempt to shout. It is possible to make your points without shouting.

  Try also not to speak too fast or mumble words. Having a clear and easy to hear voice helps in communicating with your spouse.

- **Avoid theatrics:** Do not whine, cry or wail or gesticulate violently. It is a turnoff. It creates the impression that you are a victim and your spouse, the villain. For some, the minute you begin to cry or become emotional, the conversation ends and communication will cease. While you may find yourself hurt and tearful, take control of your emotions and calmly get across your message. Avoid the following:

a. Crying
b. Wailing
c. Sulking
d. Whining
e. Throwing tantrums
f. Mournful looks
g. Lamenting
h. Gesticulating violently

- **Maintain eye contact:** Looking at your spouse and nodding occasionally gives the impression that you are listening and are interested in the conversation. Looking elsewhere creates the impression of disinterest or that you are ignoring your spouse.

CHAPTER FOUR

IN THE BEDROOM

"The problem with communication ... is the illusion that it has been accomplished". - George Bernard Shaw

The one place that communication almost never takes place, but each party assumes it has, is the bedroom. Couples assume they know, understand, can meet and have met each other's sexual needs!

The truth however is that this is rarely so. Communication in the bedroom is very vital to the marriage. A marriage may survive with lack of communication in the bedroom, but they will not enjoy the full purpose of God's plan for sex in marriage. This may inevitably lead to extra-marital affairs due to frustration. There should be no shame in talking to your spouse in the bedroom. Sex should be discussed as frankly and honestly as any other topic.

The whole purpose of sex is that it should be pleasurable and the receiver is the one who decides what is pleasurable to him or her. Therefore, each party should let the other know their likes and dislikes and not assume the other would know. Indeed it is possible to have been married for many years and still not know how to please one's spouse in the bedroom.

For a couple to have effective communication in the bedroom, they must be able to:

- **Create a convenient time to talk about sex**- The main purpose is to be open with each other and feel unashamed enough to talk about sex. While you may never really set aside "sex talk time", it is imperative that talking about sex should not be ignored, evaded and/or dismissed by either you or your spouse. Sex talk between both parties may come up anytime. At such times, you are able to discover how your spouse views sex which is almost in direct correlation to how he/she will be during love making. You must be open about sex with your spouse.

  Talking about it promotes lack of inhibition and creates a bonding that makes it easier for both of you to talk about other issues. There may also be times where you may need to communicate your view about your spouse's sexuality. A good time would naturally be after lovemaking. Anything said before, which may be developmental may spoil the mood and may cause embarrassment. In order to pass on your dislikes, it is very important that you start with letting your spouse know what you liked and how the lovemaking was for you.

- **Schedule dates (this should not stop spontaneity)** - Having a sex calendar helps in ensuring that the couple are satisfying each other. It is a way of reaching a compromise with regards to frequency. Often times, we find out that each party in a relationship has his/her own idea as to frequency of love making which results in disagreements. Scheduling creates the balance and ensures that the partner with the high sex drive is not being starved while the one with the lower sex drive is able to prepare both emotionally and physically for the sex.

In addition to this, the partner with the higher sex drive will not be in a position whereby he/she is seen as always asking for sex and getting turned down. There is an embarrassment that sometimes comes with being turned down by one's partner, which is usually what translates into anger and disagreements in the home.

- **Agree on timing-** Timing is also important in the sex life of a couple. This is usually dependent on the sleeping habits of the individuals in the relationship. A man may be an early bird while the wife on the other hand likes to sleep late, therefore waking up his wife to make love may be viewed as an insensitive act by the wife and invoke anger.

  Another instance may be when one partner may have; either worked late, is tired or indisposed, which will invariably not permit such a person to work with the timing of the other partner. Due consideration must be given to your spouse before attempting to make love.

- **Trying out new things-** If you are open to and are interested in trying out new techniques and styles, it is best to communicate such desires to your spouse. You must not assume that your spouse will not be a supportive and willing partner. It is common knowledge that rigidity is a turnoff and will ultimately lead to disinterest.

  You must be willing to encourage your spouse to explore. While this does not negate some boundaries for spiritual reasons, your willingness to participate or introduce new styles, will keep communication lines open and improve your sex life. Reading books and materials will ensure you are up to date.

- **Orgasms-** While it may be easy to know if a man has had an orgasm or not; it is not that easy with a woman and sadly, a lot of women do not experience orgasm and are suffering in silence.

    More often than not, a woman fakes orgasm and fails to inform her man that she did not experience orgasm. It is important to communicate this information so that you can both look for ways to rectify the situation in order for the enjoyment to be mutual.

- **Speak out if not enjoyable-** There are times that for various reasons sex is not enjoyable. It may be because one or both party is tired or emotionally detached. At times too, it may also be due to the existence of an unresolved issue. While make-up sex is good, it must not be used to cover up issues that need resolving.

- **Tell your spouse if it hurts-** Why grit your teeth and pray that it's over soon when you can enjoy sex? Communicating to your spouse how you feel may be the deciding factor in whether you enjoy your sex life or not. Your spouse may not know that you are hurting unless you communicate your pain and/or discomfort.

    There are times whereby the woman is too dry so much so that sex hurts. There is no way the other party can know if the one experiencing pain does not speak out. Do speak out as communicating your feelings may help in setting things right.

- **Talk during sexual intercourse to let your spouse know if it feels good**- Communication during sex is a good way to improving your sex life as well as giving each other pleasure. There are places that your spouse will touch which will give you intense pleasure. These are discoveries that will help if you inform your partner. Knowing how to please each other is the key to mutual sexual pleasure. Feel free to tell your spouse where you want him/her to touch.

  You should give feedback after sex. Without feedback, no one improves and lack of feedback is the reason so many couples still experience bad sex. If it was good for you, say it. Compliment your spouse. Everyone likes compliments. Communicating your pleasure will encourage your spouse to do better. If it wasn't good, you may say so too. However, you must bear in mind that it is not what you say that matters but how you say it.

- **Let your spouse know your fantasies (if any)** - You may have fantasies. Let your spouse know. These may be fantasies you have had for years or suddenly discovered. At times, you may see someone other than your spouse either; exhibit some behaviour or wear an outfit that you find incredibly sexy.

  Do let your spouse know as he/she may be able to play it out. Ignoring or laughing out your spouse's fantasies is dangerous and may lead to resentment as well as infidelity.

- **Be open and honest**- Honesty is very vital in any relationship. You must be honest with your spouse. Usually, what we say is not the problem. How we say it is. While being open and honest, we must be tactful. Delivery is very important. *"Say what you mean but don't say it mean"*.

- **Never talk down on your spouse with regards to his/ her sexual preference**-Sexual differences differ just as individuals do. Our preferences are also borne out of our spiritual and/or social background as well as where, when, who and how we were introduced to sex. While this may be a drawback if this knowledge is a wrong one, it is what your spouse knows and believes in.

  Talking down your spouse on his/her preference, will therefore be akin to mocking his/her background. If you are not comfortable with your spouse's sexual preference or you believe it's warped, the only way to change or influence it is for both of you to seek counselling. Who knows, you might be the one who needs counselling.

- **Do not laugh at your spouse in the bedroom**- While you can laugh *with* your spouse in the bedroom, you should not laugh *at* your spouse. Laughing *at* is a form of ridicule and what this does is to put your spouse in a position of embarrassment.

  If you must crack a joke, make sure you both understand and recognise the punch line. Laughing for no reason is also a no - no as it might be misconstrued.

- **Do not make fun of your spouse's body**- Learn to accept your spouse's body. It is important to know and realise we all do not have the same body type, shape or metabolism. Some of us eat everything in sight and still remain skinny while others barely eat but will be on the big side. Also, we all go through different experiences in life and may sometimes have the effect on our body structure. Making fun of your spouse's body will make your spouse embarrassed.

This feeling will worsen if done at the point of intimacy. Communicating your concerns must be done with tact and definitely not during sex. A good time is when you are both relaxed. You may suggest you go for work-outs later. Working out together will pass on to your spouse that you love him/her but are willing to go through the process of losing weight together.

WORDS TO COMMUNICATE BEFORE SEX

There are indeed words to communicate with your partner *before* sexual intimacy which also serves as a form of foreplay. For a woman, sex begins in the morning. Do not wait until evening to start the intimacy process. You may tell your spouse or send any of the following via text. They serve as an indication of promises of what is to come. If you are wise enough to communicate intimately with your spouse from the beginning of the day, you will find a very willing partner at the end of the day and enjoy a fulfilled sexual experience:

    a. *"I love you."*
    b. *"I need you."*
    c. *"You are beautiful."*
    d. *"You are incredibly sexy."*
    e. *"You look hot."*
    f. *"I love your body."*
    g. *"I can't wait to see you."*
    h. *"I can't wait to be with you."*

WORDS TO COMMUNICATE DURING SEXUAL INTERCOUSE

The way you communicate during the sexual act will go a long way in determining your sexual fulfilment and/or pleasure.

Communication may be in two forms: verbal or non-verbal. While words like *"I like the way you touch me there"*; *"Kiss my ear, breast"* etc. will communicate pleasure, so also would non-verbal acts like placing your hands on your partner's and guiding it, as well as *"ooh's and aah's"* will convey pleasure:

- *"This is wonderful."*
- *"I am in heaven right now."*
- *"This feels so good."*
- *"Touch me here."*
- *"I love your body."*

WORDS TO COMMUNICATE AFTER SEX

There are certain words that you need to communicate with your spouse after sex to encourage him/her. The whole purpose is to find something your spouse did well (it should not be all that bad). It is important not to tell lies about how good your spouse is or how he/she is the best you have ever been with. The following words may be used:

- *"Thanks for a wonderful time."*
- *"I love the way you make me feel."*
- *"That was wonderful."*
- *"We need a rematch."*
- *"You blow my mind."*
- *"Love you, love you, love you."*

CHAPTER FIVE

ABOUT YOUR CHILDREN

"Behold, children are a heritage from the LORD, the fruit of the womb is a reward. Like arrows in the hand of a warrior, so are the children of one's youth. Happy is the man who has his quiver full of them; they shall not be ashamed, but shall speak with their enemies in the gate." Psalms 127:3-5 NKJV

A child is a gift from God. We are caretakers and God owns them. The way and manner we communicate or do not communicate with each other as a couple will not only help shape how they will turn out in life, it may also affect how they relate in their own relationships. Coming to an agreement about your children is very important in every home.

I have often times had to mediate between couples who have failed to communicate with each other about their children. While some of the decisions may look or sound trivial or inconsequential, it isn't if it's important to the other party in the relationship. Neglecting or avoiding discussing the children and each person's expectations will invariably breed anger and distrust which will be destructive to the home.

A couple should discuss and agree on the following:

- **Number of children to have**- This decision as simply as it sounds, is still one of the decisions couples take for granted but it does cause a lot of problems in the home. If a man believes he is only able to cater for two kids and the wife feels three kids is a better number, chances are that if she gets pregnant with a third child, the husband may feel tricked and bitter. This may also breed bitterness between the couple.

- **Spacing of the children**- Child spacing is very important in the life of a couple and for the proper nurturing of a child, it is advisable and recommended so that the parents can be in the right position financially, spiritually and emotionally. In addition to this, it is better to allow a child enjoy his/her childhood as a baby before introducing another brother/sister thereby shifting attention from the older child which may inadvertently lead to neglect or "*forcing*" the child to grow up too quickly.

- **What names to give the children**- Parents are often very sentimental about the names they give a child. It is usually a name of a place, person or thing deemed very important to them. While you can give your child any name you want save for a few names which are banned, the couple must agree with each other, who names the child and in what order. Also important is communicating what circumstance a child will be named after and who in the couple's extended family is in the position to name the child. If all of the above has been communicated, it will help prevent arguments or strife.

Once the children start coming, couples must communicate on the following:

- **School to attend**- Communicating your idea of a good school and your preference for the school that best exemplifies this to your spouse is important in any relationship. There are times you may like a school but not be able to afford the fees. Reaching an agreement with your spouse regarding the schools your child will attend putting into cognisance affordability of fees and the values the child will inculcate will be great for your child as well as your relationship.

- **Friends to keep**- It is important that you decide what values you expect your child's friends to possess. As they will indeed be a great influence on your child(whether you believe it or not), agreeing as a couple to know more about your child's friends and their parents will give you a fair idea of the type of values they possess. For example, if your child has a friend who looks down on the less privileged, surely you will need to ensure that your child severs such relationships.

- **Future plans**- What are the plans you have for your child, have you communicated it to your spouse and are you both in agreement? These are the questions you need to ask each other as couples. As you are both responsible for the child, taking unilateral decisions without consulting the other is not only disrespectful but mean. Definitely, your spouse may have a different opinion or approach to the issues but as you are aware that you both mean well for your child, it will be an opportunity to look at all the pros and cons of the situation at hand so that you can give your child the best.

- **Reaching a Compromise-** While deliberating on important decisions for your child, you must be willing to reach a compromise. It is important that you both understand you are on the same side- you want the best for your child. The only thing that differs is that you both may have different definitions and/or understanding of what "best" is. When in conflict with each other, it is best not to use the child as a pawn. Also, you have to agree to disagree and come to a decision with the child's interest in mind. At such a critical stage, it is not about you or who wins or loses. It's about your child's future.

- **Check with each other before giving the child(ren) a go-ahead-** Children can indeed be crafty and/or manipulative and we have all gone through this stage of childhood at one time or the other. A child may attempt to outsmart the parents by making a request with one parent and once he/she doesn't get a favourable response, try the other parent who may then give a go ahead.

    This has for years been a major cause of conflict between couples as it's seen by the one who was first asked as a direct dismissal of his/her orders while the truth is that it is really the consequence of lack of communication between the couple. You should check with your spouse before giving a go-ahead on any request. Another way to address it is to ask, *"What did Daddy/Mummy say?"* This will give you an indication of what your spouse's stand is on the matter.

CHAPTER SIX

WITH THE CHILDREN

"You shall teach them diligently to your children, and shall talk of them when you sit in your house, when you walk by the way, and when you lie down, and when you rise up". Deuteronomy 6:7 NKJV

When a couple begin to raise children, it is very important to build relationships with each child. We have a responsibility to teach our children. Every child comes into the world dependent on the parents to learn speech, culture, social behaviour, spirituality etc. and what we teach them or fail to teach will be imbibed.

Children are like sponges and will soak up whatever they see, hear or watch you do. Each child is also created and born differently; therefore a parent may have to use different means and modes of communication.

To be able to communicate with each child, the following must be in place:

- **You must recognise your child as unique and a gift from God**- Just like no two pregnancies are exactly the same, so are your children. Even twins don't necessarily have the same character or behaviour. It is important that you recognise that your child is unique and different from everyone else. He or She is "*fearfully and wonderfully made*". God created your child for a purpose and it is that purpose that you have a responsibility to guide your child to discover.

- **You must not compare your child with the siblings or anyone else**- Comparing your child with that of your sibling or another child will destroy your child's confidence and possibly his/her future. While you may do it in good faith; believing that it will gear up the child to do as well as the sibling and possibly better; the reverse is usually the reality. A child who is constantly criticised and compared with others will have no drive to do better and unfortunately the resulting effect will be- "*the more the child is criticised and compared, the worse the child becomes*". Such a child will invariably feel unloved and withdraw into him/herself.

- **You must know your child**- In order to know your child; you must spend time together. It is indeed during those times that you are able to gather information about your child. This information includes your child's thoughts, friends they keep, places they go to etc.

- **You must be friends first**- Your child should see you as a friend and not an enemy. If you are perceived as a friend, you will be privy to some privileged information. You must demonstrate that you are on their side and anything you do is for their good. If you are going to be a friend, you must also stick to friend's rules. Friends don't tell on each other. You must also be able to keep promises.

- **You must also be a parent**- Being a friend is good but you must not also fail to be a parent. While you will be privy to a lot of information as a friend to your child, you will have to take on your parental role in giving the right advice, reprimand when necessary and give the right punishment if and as at when due.

One of the major challenges in building and/or cultivating a relationship with one's child is when the parent himself/herself did not have such a relationship with their parents; therefore he is unable to pass on anything.

At such times, the very best way to go about it is to read books and gather godly information that will aid the process.

DO:

- **Make time for individual *"Just you & I"* moments with each child**- Make sure you create time to yourselves. While it is desirable that you schedule dates and go out with your child, if time is a constraint; time spent together in the home, in their room, in the kitchen during cooking will amount to something. You must never be too busy for your child.

- **Switch off your phone and discourage interruptions**- Taking phone calls in between private conversations may communicate to the other party that you do not consider your conversation important. It will also distract you from the conversation and cause you to lose your trail of thought. The best approach is to either switch off your phone or put it on silent.

- **Try as much as possible to make it informal and as friendly as possible otherwise it will be a fruitless exercise**- Your conversation time should not be formal otherwise your child will clam up. You will not be able to communicate. You must come across to your child as fun so informal meetings or outings will most likely get more from your child than anything formal.

- **Tell a few funny stories of your own about when you were a child to diffuse/dispel distrust from your child**- You may also tell a few stories of yours as a child to warm your child up to you. Telling your stories will only let your child know that you were once a child like him/her.

- **80/20 rule** - Listen more. The ratio is four times more than you speak and also think twice before you respond. You may be able to pick a thing or two from your child's stories about his/her friends. Learn to keep quiet and listen. Do not respond without thinking it through twice. Listening will definitely let you know more about the speaker.

- **Communicate Boundaries**- Ever heard of the saying: "*Where there is no law, there is no sin*"? You need to pass across to your children house rules. It doesn't matter what happens in the neighbour's houses or their friends. They have to understand that they live by the rules you give them and not by others rules. This is what is referred to as upbringing. Lack of it brings confusion to the child as they will be exposed to different types of behaviour from their friends, peers and neighbours and be unsure of what is right or wrong. Your child must know and respond when you say no or yes.

DO NOT:

- **Shout/Scream your child down**- Allow your child to speak rather than shout him/her down. You will be able to have access to a child's thoughts once you give room for speech. Shouting/screaming a child down is the fastest way to block conversation. If the child has reasons or explanations, let them be voiced out. It will give you a clearer picture of who your child is and the values that have been imbibed.

- **Call your child names**- Calling a child various unprintable names will do no good for the child. Name calling makes the child lose confidence and feel less human. There is also the risk of false accusation which makes a child more defiant and inclined to misbehave. The child takes on the attitude of *"after all, they already think I am like that"*. Refrain from using negative words. Remember; the power of life and death is in the tongue. Even, if you have reasons to believe your child has/is doing badly, continue to give positive affirmations and *"call things that are not as though they were"* Romans 4:17.

- **Use information your child gave you against him/her**- Once in a while, our children open up to us and give us information about what is going on in their generation. This should not be stored up as ammunition to be used later otherwise, such a child will clam up and you will never get anything from him/her again. Whatever information that needs to be acted upon must be done with love and in a manner that will not come across to the child that you are judging their conduct.

- **Ignore your child when he/she has something to say-** If you have a child who is willing to tell you anything, please make time out to listen. Do not ignore your child. Your taking time out to listen may be a lifeline for you and/or your child. Do not ever be too busy to listen.

A child who is frequently talked down on by the parent will ultimately lose respect for the parents. He/she will become very angry and may lash out against the world. The word of God enjoins us to watch out for this. *"Fathers, do not provoke your children to anger, but bring them up in the discipline and instruction of the Lord"*. Ephesians 6:4 NASB

WORDS TO COMMUNICATE TO YOUR CHILD

- *"You are the best."*
- *"You can do it."*
- *"You are fearfully and wonderfully made."*
- *"You will be the head and not the tail."*
- *"You will excel."*
- *"You will be the first and not the last."*
- *"You are made for signs and wonders."*
- *"You are a generation changer."*
- *"You are very smart."*
- *"You are beautiful in every single way."*
- *"We are proud of you."*

WORDS NOT TO SAY TO YOUR CHILDREN

- *"Useless child."*
- *"Irresponsible child."*
- *"You were a mistake."*

- *"We should not have had you."*
- *"You are dumb."*
- *"You have no brains."*
- *"You are the only different one in this house."*
- *"You always disappoint us."*
- *"We are ashamed of you."*
- *"Your brother/sister is better than you."*
- *"Why is it always you that messes up?"*
- *"You are not like me at all."*

CHAPTER SEVEN

RELATIVES

W ho are your relatives? They are your parents, siblings, aunts, uncles, cousins etc. You may believe that your relatives are good people and indeed they may be. However, they should not be in the position to wield an influence in your home. Your home belongs to you and your spouse.

Consider this: You have a property which has no fence and neither is there a defined landmark to indicate the parameters of your ownership. You will indeed have left your property for anyone to claim, as well as trespass and you may not be in the position to sue for trespass as there is nothing to show your ownership. Strays and robbers may also come in to destroy your property.

The importance of the fence is that it is for protection of your property as well as put in place to keep trespassers and strays away. The fences of your home are the boundaries you will create. You must erect them to safeguard your home. Lack of boundaries in the home will eventually breed unstable and unhappy home.

I once had to counsel a newly wedded man. Let's call him David; David was newly married to Edna. They were yet to mark a year in marriage but it was obvious that he was terribly unhappy. He explained to me that he had thought marriage was a good cause and though he never made mention of no longer loving his wife, he found himself happier staying away from her.

As he came for counsel alone, I made attempts to find out more about him, the marriage and his reasons for getting married. This is the story he told me:

David had married Edna because he fell in love and really wanted to make a home for himself. However, he has a younger brother who he felt he was responsible for his upkeep and livelihood and so invited the brother to live with him and his newly wedded wife.

This decision did not go well with his new bride, Edna as she was neither consulted nor informed about it. Edna invariably found herself living with two men right from the beginning of her marriage when she bargained for only one.

David let me know that he was aware of some friction between his brother and his wife-Edna and had heard some concerns from his wife and her wish to have David's brother leave the house but he has made it clear to her that his brother is not going anywhere and has come to stay.

Evidently, from what David told me, Edna was very unhappy and David who she knew could take a decision which can make her happy doesn't communicate with her and has clearly informed her that there would be no change in the nearest future. Consequently, Edna in retaliation has tried all attempts to make David feel her pain. End result; a very unhappy couple. Sadly, the marriage didn't last a year.

From the above story, we can see how easy it is to have a third party ruin our relationship with our spouse. In this instance, what created the problem was the following:

a. David failed to communicate his intention to have his brother come live with them with his spouse in order for them to reach an agreement.

b. David had undue emotional attachment with his brother.

c. David failed to listen to his wife's complaints.

d. David ultimately put his relative before his spouse.

Very often we find it easier to communicate not too pleasant decisions to people we do not know. While with those we know; especially our relatives, we become emotional and may not be bold enough to take a stand on issues. We should always remember that the word of God enjoins us to leave, cleave and become one. You must leave your relatives. It might be painful but that is the prerequisite for cleaving and becoming one.

As familiar as they will try to be because they are your relatives and have known you all your life, you must create boundaries which must not be crossed. In agreement with your spouse, there must be no-go areas for both your relatives and your spouse.

HOW CAN YOU SET BOUNDARIES?

- **Become one :**
  "Therefore shall a man leave his father and his mother, and shall cleave unto his wife: and they shall be one flesh" Genesis 2:24 KJV
  The word of God says it all. You must leave your parents and cleave to your spouse. This scripture applies to both the man and the woman. While leaving in this case is definitely not abandonment or desertion, it is becoming one with your spouse so that your relatives will see and perceive that you are united.

While you will discover that your relatives will attempt different strategies and tricks to enable them have their way with you, you must always have at the back of your mind that you have left them and are now united with your spouse. Any action you take with them without your spouse's knowledge serves as a betrayal to your spouse. However difficult the situation may be, you must keep a united front with your spouse. A united front is not easily broken.

- **Non-disclosure:**
As a couple, you must decide what information you want to share with your relatives. It serves no good for the relationship if you end up sharing information that you both did not take a decision on with regards to who knows and who doesn't.

  While your relatives may be eager to learn about your spouse as the addition to the family, you have to be careful the type of information you offer. If you are in doubt, you can ask them to ask your spouse themselves. Do not disclose personal information or what you and your spouse have spoken about in private and in the confines of your home.

  Disagreements and misunderstandings must also not be disclosed as what happens in your home is not the business of your parents or siblings. Truth be told, whatever information received by your parents and/or siblings (which is usually used as ammunition against your spouse in future) are information offered by yourself. It is important to keep a rein on your tongue and keep your parents and siblings out of your home.

Naturally, there will be times where your relatives will be in your home either on a visit or a short stay. It is indeed possible to have a guest stay in your home but keep the guest out of your business.

While the word of God says that we should: *"Honour your father and your mother, that your days may be long upon the land which the LORD your God is giving you."* Exodus 20:12 NKJV; you can respect your parents but also respectfully ask that they allow you to deal with any situation in your home by yourself irrespective of the fact that they may have witnessed a thing or two.

While it is indeed possible that your relatives probably mean well and are trying to help, the reality of the situation is that your spouse may not see it that way and it will not help matters if one party feels misjudged during conflict resolution.

The trick is in creating a balance as building boundaries does not mean estrangement. Relatives can be a good source of support at various times and shutting them out completely will do no good; however you must be in control of your home.

The following are some of the information you do not necessarily need to divulge to your relatives:

- *Your spouse's age*
- *Your spouse's financial worth*
- *Your spouse's weaknesses*
- *Your spouse's past*
- *Your spouse's shortcomings*
- *Intimate details of your spouse*

The ability to keep one's relatives in check means peace for your spouse and in your home.

COMMUNICATING SET BOUNDARIES

It is one thing to set boundaries but it is another for one to be able to communicate them and how. When you and your spouse have determined the boundaries for relatives in your home, you are both responsible for notifying your relatives of the boundaries. For example, I will let my relatives know while my husband will tell his own relatives. Secondly, we both have decided that we will use the word *"we"* and not *"I"* or *"my spouse said"*.

Using *"we"* passes on the following messages to your relatives:

    a. It's a collective decision

    b. You are in agreement with the decision

    c. You intend standing by the decision

    d. You are united

Once you are able to communicate the above to your relatives, they may not like your decision, but they will respect it. What happens if you have set boundaries and you find your spouse's relative disregarding it. This is when you need wisdom from above in order not make it seem as if you are reporting your in-law (we will address in-law issues in the next chapter).

I do recall my second year of marriage....we had moved into a back flat of my mother-in-law's and was practically within her reach.

Having a very boisterous and very outgoing mother, my husband and I had communicated to each other the boundaries we wanted to keep in our home. One of our major concerns was how to keep and guard our privacy with my mother in-law a stone throw away. More so, that she is very social and always had a family or two as guest.

For the first month or so, we thought we had succeeded until my mother-in-law knocked on my door while my husband was away and brought with her an elderly man who was supposed to be a long lost uncle of my husband's to my home. She proceeded to open every room in the house showing the place off to this uncle in-law. She spared no room. She opened the bathroom, toilet, even our bedroom for the guest! I was livid but clearly handicapped as not only could I not express my displeasure, I had to keep a smiling face - after all; she was my mother-in-law.

Clearly, this was my husband's call but he was nowhere near home and had not witnessed it. By the time my husband returned, they had left and I did not know how to let him know what went on without it looking like I was telling on my mother in-law (after all, we had only been there for a month!)

I initially took a decision to sit it out and choose to believe that this habit will end as quickly as it started. However, it was not to be and the more I tried to accept it, the more strange people were brought into my home. One thing that struck me about it all was that my mother-in-law never brought anyone over when my husband was home and so I discovered that the only person who could resolve the issue at hand was my husband.

This revelation further reaffirmed my challenge-"how do I let my husband know and get him on my side?"

What did I do? I carefully and casually mentioned how my mother in-law drops by every now and then to see how I was doing. This information got him annoyed and irritated as he felt the reason she could be so frequent was because we lived so close. His reaction was all I needed as I attempted to pacify him by adding that she probably meant no harm and wanted to show me and the house off to the extended family since she usually comes over with one or two people.

He was furious. He made his way to his Mum and made a lot of fuss about how he wants his privacy and would rather not have anyone come see him at home.

I calmly explained to my mother in-law that I was just trying to pass across the information about our guest and he got unreasonably angry (there was no way I was going to let either my husband or mother-in-law know that everything was working according to plan – even though all is now in the open now). I kept a united front with my mother-in-law and we both wondered why my husband was so angry.

He made it very clear that he no longer wanted visitors. Though my mother in-law did not like this, she respected his wishes. I was happy with the decision taken and most importantly, was not blamed for it!

We can note from the above story:

- My husband and I had both reached an agreement concerning boundaries in the home, however, it was difficult for me to convey this to my mother in-law and I had to use the wisdom of God to ensure that he passes the message to his mum.

- My husband was quick to address the situation when the boundaries were crossed to ensure that there was no repeat.

- I ensured that I *"appeared"* to disagree with my husband when it involved his relatives but secretly was in agreement- this was purely a survival instinct strategy. *"The wise woman builds her house, but the foolish pulls it down with her hands" Proverbs* 14:1 NKJV. My mother in-law was convinced her son was being very irrational but had to respect his wishes concerning our home. She forgave her son quickly. It will indeed have been harder to forgive me and quickly too!

One important thing to note is that boundaries should only be communicated when crossed. It is ridiculous to write a list of boundaries and hand over to your family and friends. This is very bad for human relations. As boundaries are crossed you can gently let the person know that those are areas you will not want them to cross.

Remember that it is usually not the intent of the offending parties to cause harm or disrespect you as what is unacceptable in your home may be acceptable elsewhere; therefore you must communicate respectfully.

The only time you may be a bit firm may be if your wishes are discountenanced or dismissed, then you may also have to ask the person to stay away from your home.

CHAPTER EIGHT

IN-LAWS

"Your People Shall Be My People, and Your God, My God"-
Ruth 1:16 NKJV

Getting along with your in-laws is one major challenge that confronts every married couple. The initial meeting of a prospective spouse's relatives is usually with the anticipation and fear of how we will be received. There are concerns about our being liked or disliked. We naively believe our in- laws can't help but love us once they see how much in love we both are. Right? Wrong. The strength of your love for each other does not determine how well you will be accepted and be able to communicate with your in-laws.

Opinions(positive or negative) are sometimes formed even before the first meeting and this will indeed go a long way in shaping communication between you and your in-laws. Some of these opinions will be from information received about us and also other people's perceptions about us.

More often than not, we do not set out to hate our in-laws. On the contrary, we assume that since we have such a great relationship with our spouse, we would too with his relatives. However, that is usually not the case. What we should always remember is that we are all different and irrespective of any previous misconceptions about us, we can dispel them by treating our in-laws right. Once we have at the back of our minds that they were (and still are) a big part of our spouse's life, it will be easier to deal and communicate with our in-laws.

We must make up our minds to love our in-laws and make the most of the few minutes/hours we spend with them. It is also important that we be ourselves as it is usually a disappointment in not having our efforts to love them being reciprocated (we sometimes try too hard to please) that makes us do a 360 degree turn around and be battle ready. We must remember that going to war always brings casualties and peaceful resolution is usually far off as both parties try to score points.

We can try the following approach in communicating with our in-laws:

- **Respect them**- Your spouse's parents are and should be recognised as your parents too. You must not disrespect them under any circumstance. Respect is reciprocal and you must always try to respect both younger and older in-laws. Once you have established mutual respect, you will find it easier to communicate.

- **Show that you care**- Showing that you care about your in-law's welfare goes a long way in opening communication lines between the two of you. While you may be busy and not be in a position to make frequent visits, just calling to find out your in-laws welfare will not only pass the message across that you believe they are important to you, it will also endear you to them.

- **Learn their culture and tradition**- With the exception of couples who are from the same locale, it is important for you to learn and understand part of your in-laws culture as this will help in establishing effective communication. Do not just assume things will work out on their own; you need to make an effort.

- **Be united with your spouse**- You must keep a united front. You must work together with your spouse. Whatever you are going to say to your in-laws must be in sync. Nothing destroys an in-law relationship more than you saying one thing and their son/daughter saying another. Even if you are the one with the truth, you will be disbelieved as there is the natural assumption that their son/daughter can do no wrong. You should get your facts and stories right before volunteering any information.

  Also, decisions to be communicated must have been agreed with your spouse and any loopholes covered. Delivery will be determined by the type of news to be communicated. If it's good news, it must be communicated by the spouse that is not their child. If it's bad and/or uncomfortable news, then it's their son/daughter that will communicate the news.

- **Determine not to get angry**- While communicating with your in-laws, irrespective of how they might have spoken to you, you must determine not to get angry. Keeping a check on your emotions will help your relationship. There is no use getting upset with your in-laws because it will always be viewed differently by them which may inadvertently lead to a gang up on you. You will end up fighting so many battles that you were not aware existed as there is usually a sympathy support fighting group. Learn to mask your anger or distress. You may be able to address the situation in another way and at another time.

- **Have set boundaries and limits**- Have your set limits and boundaries. Do what you would normally do. While you may sometimes make exceptions, do not pretend or try too hard to please. It's hard to keep up. Besides if it's not what you will normally do, it will cause you discomfort and you will be on edge or under a strain.

- **No third party communication**- If you need to pass on information to your in-laws, it is wrong to go through a third party irrespective of how well you believe the person will do the job. You may arrange a time when you are able to speak to the in-law in question yourself. Address the issue in a clear respectful manner and ask if there is anything your in-laws will like you to do more of.

- **Be secure in yourself**- Be yourself, don't try to be someone else. You will probably be compared with either an ex or another person in the family. You must be confident in yourself so that you do not end up using all your energy trying to be someone else.

- **Be friendly and nice**- Make friends but don't get too close. With the exception of those who were very close friends before marrying into the family, it is advisable that one does not keep too close with your in-laws. It is usually through this act of closeness that stories and information that should not be heard are communicated.

- **Be natural**- Don't try too hard to please. While you may bend over backwards occasionally in a bid to accommodate others, putting yourself under pressure will not do you any good as there is a higher chance of you snapping than if you are doing things that are not natural.

COMMUNICATING WITH YOUR MOTHER-IN-LAW (WOMEN)

It is indeed a big mistake to treat your mother-in-law the same way you treat other in-laws. Her role as the most important woman in your spouse's life, gives her the right to be treated specially. How do you open communication lines with your mother-in-law? Find below tips that you can use:

- **Acknowledge her relevance**-You must acknowledge to yourself that she is important to your spouse. Do not try to change their close relationship overnight. You mother in-law will resist it and so would your spouse. Understand that their relationship has taken about 25-30 years (before your entrance) to build. You will have to find a way to adapt yourself to their relationship style, whether you like it or not.

  Once you can accept your mother in-law as an important aspect of your spouse's life, you will see her actions in a different light. While you may still find her a little too intrusive and may still not accept her actions, you will understand them.

- **Make friends**- You have to make friends with your mother in-law. While you may not necessarily go visiting every day or week, she is one person that you must pen down on your "to do list" to call and visit at least once a month with or without your spouse. It is important that you "keep in touch" constantly irrespective of whether your spouse does same with his/her relatives. You will find out that it is usually very easy for your in-laws to "forgive" their son/daughter little and big indiscretions but not you. More often than not, you might even be blamed for them.

You and your mother-in-law should be able to sit together and have a friendly conversation. Once you are able to understand that you are both on the same side, it is easier to be friends. However, you have to make the extra effort in ensuring that you are a friend and not an enemy as you are the one joining the family.

- **Give gifts**- These are called tangible expressions of love. If you wish to communicate effectively with your mother in-law, you must give gifts. These could range from cash gifts, food and personal effects. These items need not be expensive however, the gains will be unquantifiable.

- **Empathise with her**- You can try to put yourself in your mother in-law's shoes to understand how she feels about you. The truth is that you will probably act the same way which is the very reason mother-in-law issues still abound today though the mothers-in-law themselves had the same experience with their own mothers-in-law.

A lot of actions taken by mothers-in-law are borne out of fear of "losing" their son to someone else. More so when it is her son, losing to another woman is never a pleasant experience irrespective of in what context; which is why wives have the most issues regarding mothers-in-law.

- **Find common interest**- there must be something about your mother in-law that interests you too. You have to look for common interest and use that to bond. You may go out shopping together or even if it's to school plays. Invite her to go with you to your children's events and make out time to follow her to her friend's too. You may even schedule hair salon visits together. These are subtle ways to bond with her.

- **Be receptive towards her**- Almost all the ways you have learnt to take care of your spouse and home will elicit a different method from your mother-in-law. While she may be old fashioned and/or out of date, she did take care of your spouse, didn't she? You owe it to her to at least lend a listening ear. You may not accept her methods but you have to listen to her if you want her to listen to you too.

- **Define your boundaries**: Do let your mother in-law know in a respectful but firm manner what values you hold and what your preferences are in your home. She may attempt to tell and/or show you how her son prefers his food or the home setting. While you can acknowledge her input and thank her for it, you do not have to accept it and let her know you prefer your own way. If respectfully said, she will accept though she may not understand it, which will invariably cause a little friction but she will come around.

COMMUNICATING WITH YOUR MOTHER-IN-LAW (MEN)

Truth be told, there are not half as many men than women who have issues with their mother-in-law.

- **Create boundaries**- As a man, you must not be seen or perceived as a walk-over. A woman can smell a weak man from a mile and as weakness is unattractive to a woman; your mother- in-law will most likely treat you with disdain if she thinks you are not man enough to protect her daughter. There must be areas in your home that are no-go areas even to your mother-in-law. You must put your foot down if need be and she will definitely fall in line. Remember you are the man of the house.

- **Show respect and love**- Be respectful and show love. Let her know that you appreciate the fact that she is the mother of the love of your life. Be quick to apologise if need be.

- **Give money**-Learn to give money howbeit little. Women like money. Don't bother with gifts unless you are still going to add money to it. If you don't want to give randomly, you can decide to do a monthly stipend. Remember, it is not so much the amount that matters but the gesture as well as consistency.

- **Watch what you say**- Your conversation should be closely guarded. Do not speak loosely. Remember words can be reprocessed and your words may be quoted out of context or used against you. Watch your words.

- **Treat her like your mother**- Culturally in this part of the world; it is believed that when you get married, you inherit another mother-your spouse's mother. She is not your enemy. Learn to forgive her, even when she upsets you or overstep her boundaries. Sometimes you may need to overlook her faults by attributing her excesses to old age respectfully. You will find out that you will get along better.

WORDS NOT TO SAY TO YOUR IN-LAWS:

- *"You are not wanted here."*
- *"What did you contribute to my spouse's life?"*
- *"The battle line has been drawn."*
- *"I know your story."*
- *"I did not marry you; I married your son/daughter."*
- *"Don't come to this house again."*
- *"I hate you."*
- *"I can't stand you."*
- *"My husband/wife loves me more than you."*

CHAPTER NINE

FRIENDS, NEIGHBOURS & HIRED HELP

"Bad human communication leaves us less room to grow".
Rowan D Williams

O nce married, you have to understand that your relationship with your unmarried friends will take a different turn. Without necessarily making a conscious effort to reduce communication, you will discover that you may not just have the time. It becomes harder as you will be otherwise occupied trying to understand and fit into your new role as a wife/husband. You may also find out that your priorities change and the conversations that you used to have with your unmarried friends become less important. This will probably create awkward moments if your friend is unmarried and you may be placed in a position whereby you try not to offend your unmarried friend.

Definitely, in order to have success in your marriage, your communication rate with your unmarried friends will need to change. While it is not advisable that you sever your relationships, (except for bad influence), you will definitely need to reduce time spent communicating with them.

Consider the following story:

Mrs. A just got married. She used to be part of a group of friends who were party goers, fun loving girls. The usual trend is for friends to visit or call each other and update one another on the status of their love life and experiences. On one of the days, Mr. A overheard part of their conversation and he was not happy. The various thoughts that ran through his head got him thinking that if these were the kind of friends his wife kept, then she must be capable of same. His thoughts were that while he was willing to forgive his spouse anything she did before they got married; continuous and constant communication between his wife and her friends may encourage her to embrace the old way of life. He resolved that she must sever communication lines with her friend if she wished to keep her marriage intact.

When you find yourself in a situation whereby you have a few unmarried friends and you are married, it is the strength of the relationship that will keep you going. You must remember that friendship is not about the frequency of your communication but how strong your relationship is.

There are friends you only see once a year but you are able to catch up on important things and it will be as if you were never apart. Note the following:

- Your spouse should be your number one friend.
- Not every friend remains a friend once your status changes.
- Not every friend should follow you to the next level.
- Your real friends will understand your new status and respect it.

- You do not need too many friends.
- You should not tell your friend intimate details about your spouse.
- It is the quality of your friendship that counts; not the quantity.

Neighbours

Your neighbours are the people with whom you live in close proximity. While it is not unusual for you to cultivate a close relationship with one or more of them, it is important to remember that there should be some limitations to your closeness.

The main challenge in being too close and divulging all the information about your home is that it may lead to issues like envy, jealousy, unhealthy competition as well strife. It could also lead to your being on the disadvantage if all your weaknesses or that of your spouse has been made bare to outsiders.

Be careful what you tell your neighbour about yourself, spouse or children. Always remember that they also have close friends they confide in and you run the risk of having the whole neighbourhood know about your private matters.

- Remember neighbours move houses and so do you; therefore, there is a chance you may meet later in the future. It will be hard to correct some of the information such a neighbour has.
- Keep your voice and conversations at a moderate level when speaking in your home. This is most important when you live in a neighbourhood where the houses are built closely to one another. "*The walls have ears*" and part of those ears are neighbours. You owe yourself a duty to watch what you say as well as what they can hear.

Domestic Help

These are those who work for you or your spouse. They are people who will be in such close proximity that they will probably see or hear some of the interactions between you and your family. While they may be in the know and be witnesses, it is usually safer and better not to confide or have conversations about your home.

History has shown time and time again that speaking to a hired help is a bad idea as they usually end up cashing in on the opportunity either by divulging your information to a soft sell magazine or writing a tell all book and/or blackmail.

Remember:

- **Keep it professional**- Your hired staff will leave someday and while some of them become closer than family and it turns out well, it's best to keep them what they are- hired staff

- **Resist the urge to "confide" in your hired help**- They probably have guessed anyway. It's best not to confirm their suspicions.

- **Retain respectability**- While you may encourage open communications with your hired help, you should always balance it with some boundaries. This will ensure that your master/servant relationship remains intact. There shouldn't be any doubt as to who the master is in your relationship with the hired help. Giving information about your spouse may encourage your hired help disrespect them. Do not encourage them to feed you back also. This habit will not help your relationship as you will find out that there will always be information to give. Furthermore, in an attempt to keep you fully updated, fabrications may begin to occur. None of these will enhance your relationship with your spouse.

CHAPTER TEN

FAMILY

"If you as parents cut corners, your children will too. If you lie, they will too. If you spend all your money on yourselves and tithe no portion of it for charities, colleges, churches, synagogues, and civic causes, your children won't either. And if parents snicker at racial and gender jokes, another generation will pass on the poison adults still have not had the courage to snuff out"- Marian Wright Edelman

How often have we heard the phrase, "*it is a family tradition*"? Usually it passes on from generation to generation without necessarily understanding the origin. This of course shows that the quickest and fastest way to get a message across as a family is to spend time together. It does the family no good if one party is consistently absent. The absence of a mother or father may in itself confuse a child.

As a parent, we can only build relationships with our children by being present in their lives. With your presence as a parent, you will be in the position to notice their behavioural trend and ask the right questions. Also, your presence will also help in building trust and promote bonding as opposed to your child dealing with a complete stranger.

I was once told of the story of a man who was always not available at home due to work pressure. He would be away for weeks and show up for a few days. Things got to a head when his one-year old daughter began to talk and call him *"Uncle"*. He realised that he needed to set for himself the right priorities.

In order to avoid the above situation, you must:

- **Be available:** With the constant hustle and bustle of life and in a bid to make ends meet, we tend to get ourselves overworked. This invariably puts us in a position whereby it is our children we neglect or leave their care in the hands of nannies. As parents, we must be able to schedule or arrange our timing in order to be available for those important moments in a child's life. A child who is neglected or left in the hands of nannies will imbibe their values and beliefs which may indeed be totally different from yours. Also you run the risk of making your child a stranger to yourself.

    Additionally, it is important to also note that the fact that you are all in the same area and/or vicinity does not mean you are communicating. Communication will only open up when you create an opportunity for it. In other words, you must be available to talk and listen. It is indeed a bad sign if you are in the habit of cutting short members of your family. Words not to say to your family members:
    a. *"I am busy right now."*
    b. *"Can we talk later?"*
    c. *"Not now."*
    d. *"You talk too much."*
    e. *"I am sick and tired of talking/listening to you."*
    f. *"I hate the sound of your voice."*

g. *"You are disturbing me."*
h. *"What do you want?"*
i. *"Can I have some peace and quiet in this house?"*

- **Get rid of distractions**: It is hard to concentrate fully on what someone else is saying when there is something else competing for your attention. Best way to go about communication fully is to ask each family member to spare you a few minutes by either switching off the television, radio or iPod. Cell phones and games can be placed on silent while you enjoy family time together. You may pass this to your kids that it serves as showing a sign of respect for one another.

- **Making use of available moments and places**: Communicating with your family does not always have to be a formal affair. You may seize any opportunity that comes your way. One of the ways is to encourage each member of the family to talk either in the car when driving out together or in the children's room. You may use subtle ways to ask for each member of the family's opinion.

    Just be sure that any topic up for discussion should be one everyone can talk about. Another way could be during the course of playing indoor games. These games could be monopoly, scrabble or Nintendo. Indoor games are a good strategy to have a glimpse and understand how members of your family handle pressure, winning and losing.

- **Take meals as a family**: While the hustle and bustle of life may hinder a family from having all meals together, there must be a conscious effort for the family to try as much as possible to take at least a meal together either once a day or week as time permits. It will be an opportunity for everyone to talk about the events of the day and also what is happening in individual lives.

- **Encourage family traditions**: As much as you can, make the Sunday church service a tradition for the family. Ensure that you drive to church together and in the same car (if one car will take all). Another way is to schedule family vacations together. By going to interesting places as a family, you create history and bond together which you will be able to reminisce on in future.

As you build your home, you will find out that you will have ways of communicating that will be peculiar to your home. With time, you will discover that you have grown as a family enough to be able to read and understand each other's body language and mannerisms. This will eventually develop into a relationship whereby non-verbal words will be used more often than verbal. A look from a spouse to the other, parent to child as a way of communicating creates a bond that is not easily broken. It will also communicate volumes and serve as way of passing across messages when in public or in the midst of strangers.

Having said all, it is evident that while there are many types of ways to communicate, we as individuals will have a certain way we prefer to be communicated to. Therefore we should strive to discover how to communicate to whoever we are attempting to reach. We must learn how to say what we mean but not say it mean.

AFTERWORD

"The colossal misunderstanding of our time is the assumption that insight will work with people who are unmotivated to change. Communication does not depend on syntax, or eloquence, or rhetoric, or articulation but on the emotional context in which the message is being heard. People can only hear you when they are moving toward you, and they are not likely to when your words are pursuing them. Even the choicest words lose their power when they are used to overpower. Attitudes are the real figures of speech". - Edwin Friedman

There are various factors that hinder communication among couples. As communication is between two people - the speaker and the listener, the husband and the wife - they both have a responsibility to ensure effective communication. Communication is both ways. It is not the responsibility of one party alone.

When either one of the parties involved fails to keep to his/her side of the bargain; that is when there is either no communication or it is said to have broken down.

**Actions that may serve as effective communication killer:
Actions by the man:**

- **Religion:** The man of the house proclaims headship at every opportunity. A man is and has indeed been ordained by God as the head of the home. Head? Yes. Dictator? No. The man being the head of the home is God ordained. It is not a role given by man, so a man does not need to impress on his wife at every opportunity his headship.

> *"Wives submit yourselves unto your own husbands, as unto the Lord. For the husband is head of the wife, even as Christ is head of the church; and he is the saviour of the body. Therefore as the church is subject to Christ, so let wives be to their own husbands in everything. Husbands love your wife as Christ also loved the church and gave himself for it . . . So ought men to love their wives as their own bodies. He that loveth his wife loveth himself. For no man ever yet hated his own flesh but nourisheth and cherisheth it, even as the Lord the church . . . For this cause shall a man leave his father and mother and shall be joined unto his wife, and they two shall be one flesh."* Ephesians 5:22, 28-31KJV

A man who consistently insists that he is the head of the home will block communication lines. Truth is that a man who feels the need to remind his spouse constantly of his headship has actually lost the headship. He will not encourage his spouse to communicate freely. The man is the head of the home, not a dictator.

While addressing issues concerning the home, a wise man should of necessity ask for his wife's opinion or suggestion concerning any matter before taking a decision. Each party will lay down his/her views, which will be deliberated upon. A wife must submit to the final decision taken by the man. It is often said, *"Two heads are better than one".*

- **Always right, never wrong attitude:** There are men who have taken on the attitude of always right, never wrong. Such a man will not open or encourage effective communication in the home just because he feels he knows it all. God is the only one who is all knowledgeable. Learning is a continuous progressive act. We never stop learning; therefore a man must be willing to accept that he is not infallible. No man created by God is. Sometimes we are wrong and other times we are right. A man must be willing to admit when he is wrong and seek help.

- **Loveless union:** A man who no longer demonstrates his love for his spouse will not be in the position to communicate effectively. His spouse will indeed be too bitter and frustrated to be willing to participate in any form of communication. Such couples will inadvertently end up as "co-tenants". They will live in the same house but will be living different lives.

  Communication will have reduced to zero and only words like "*hello*"; "*good morning*" etc. will exist between them. Love is a much-needed prerequisite to effective communication. A woman who is not secure in her husband's love will not be willing to submit herself to any form of communication with him.

- **Verbal and Physical Abuse:** a man, who verbally, emotionally, and physically abuses his wife, may very well have closed the door to any form of effective communication between the two. These loveless acts are not quickly or easily forgotten especially when you are the recipient.

A woman, who is in an abusive relationship, will not communicate with her spouse. She will either discountenance his words in defiance or in retaliation. The fear of being hit again does not serve as a deterrent; which is part of the reasons that made those in abusive relationships to continue to stay.

- **Unavailability:** Being away from your spouse under the guise of work or duty will definitely have an impact on your communication level. It will indeed be difficult to keep you in the loop as a lot would have happened which events may have overtaken before you are available for a talk. The danger of a man's unavailability is that both of you may inadvertently end up living separate lives which is dangerous for the survival of any relationship.

- **Culture/Tradition:** There are some cultures that the woman is only seen and not heard. Such culture will not allow open and effective communication between couples, as the woman will not be able to contribute anything to the home in the form of advice or training of children.

Actions by the woman:

- **Lack of Submission:** While a woman is indeed the co-pilot in the home, she should always remember; *"There cannot be two masters on a ship"*. One person has to take control and take charge. While a man may sometimes defer to his wife, the woman should not battle or nag it out of him.

A woman who refuses to submit to her husband is, for one, going against the word of God, as well as putting herself into danger. If a man is busy engaged in internal battles with his wife, then he will not be able to conquer the world. A godly woman will submit to her man even though she may not fully agree with his idea or method. Arguments are the number one communication killers as it wears out both parties and nothing is resolved. It becomes more of back to square one. Jonathan Swift said, *"Argument is the worst sort of conversation"*.

- **Disrespect:** The greatest thing a man needs is to be respected by his wife. If, as a woman, you continuously disrespect your man, he will not be willing to have a conversation with you. A woman who disrespects her man causes him shame and a man will always move away from anything that causes him shame. Some of the ways a woman can disrespect her man are as follows:
  - a. Ridicule him in the presence of her family and friends
  - b. Shout him down in the presence of their children
  - c. Tell intimate stories about him to friends
  - d. Highlight his short comings

- **Knowing when to talk:**
  "Remember not only to say the right thing in the right place, but far more difficult still, to leave unsaid the wrong thing at the tempting moment."-Benjamin Franklin
  In order to communicate effectively, a woman must read and understand her man to know when to approach him on some issues. Approaching a man when he is tired, hungry or about to watch his club play a match will most probably

yield no positive result. A woman has to study her man enough to know when to grasp his full attention.

There is nothing wrong in asking when it will be okay to have a talk with your spouse. This should elicit a response that will make him take out time to hear you out. Scheduling "talk time" is also good for the relationship. A good time may be early hours of the morning when you are both together.

- **Knowing when not to talk:**
  "Set a guard over my mouth, O LORD; keep watch over the door of my lips". Psalm 141:3 NASB
  There are lots of times in a relationship that talking is not necessary. A wise woman will know when to keep quiet. It is an unwise woman that will comment on everything. The downside of commenting on every issue is that the woman will run the risk of either being called a nag or not taken seriously.

  Sometimes you must *"play the fool"* as a woman. Learn to keep a hold on your tongue. Pretend you didn't see what just happened. Most times when you keep quiet, the other party will not anticipate your next move and you will become unreadable. In order to be taken seriously during communication, be careful not to express lots of loose talk.

- **Choose your words:**
  Words are like eggs; once broken, can never be picked back. It is important that you choose the right words to communicate with your spouse. Your words must speak life and not death. A woman should carefully pick and weigh her words before delivery. There are some words that should not be used with a man i.e. words that affect his ego,

manhood, self-respect etc. Words like the following should be avoided at all costs:

a. *"You are not a man."*
b. *"You are a weak man."*
c. *"Mr. Jones is a better man."*
d. *"You should be ashamed of yourself."*

There is no conversation between a couple that is a waste of time. Conversations are good for the growth of the union. It should be seen as another opportunity to learn more about your partner. Communication is also an opportunity to grow together. If you have meaningful conversations with one another, it is an indication of a healthy union. Marriages end and homes break when communication breaks down. You must ensure it does not happen to you.

WHAT TO DO TO OPEN COMMUNICATION LINES

- **Words of Affirmation**
  "Appreciation can make a day, even change a life. Your willingness to put it into words is all that is necessary"-Margaret Cousins
  In order to ensure you have open communication lines in the home, it is important to use words of affirmation. Words of affirmation encourage and appreciate the recipient. Its use creates a healthy environment for growth of the relationship. You may use encouraging or appreciative words daily. You do not need to wait until your spouse does something major.
  Saying thank you for just being there gives the recipient a sense of belonging and you are less likely to find it easy to

communicate other issues. From what I have gathered from a lot of couples I have been privileged to counsel, it is not so much of what the other party complains about that annoys but for the fact that he/she has never given or said a word of appreciation to the other party. The following words can be used:

a. *"Thank you."*
b. *"I appreciate you."*
c. *"You are wonderful."*
d. *"You can do it."*
e. *"You are smart."*
f. *"You are the best."*

- **Be interested**

"The secret of happiness is this: let your interests be as wide as possible, and let your reactions to the things and persons that interest you be as far as possible friendly rather than hostile."
Bertrand Russell

Show an interest in your surroundings. Taking a closer look will most probably give you an opportunity to notice when things have gone wrong or are not the way it usually is. Then you are able to ask questions, which will open communication lines.

Total disinterest and or aloofness by one party are some of the reasons couples do not bother to communicate with each other. I once had a conversation with a friend about my hair. I wanted to change my hairstyle but wasn't sure my husband would like it. She was shocked that my husband would notice the change.

She bitterly told me that even if she placed her shoes on her head, her husband would not notice anything different.

This was clearly a situation my friend did not like but had come to accept. Showing an interest is not only a sign that you care but also an indication that you are not living in a world of your own and are interested in someone else's welfare. The word of God says: *"Each of you should look not only to your own interests, but also to the interests of others"* Philippians 2:4(NIV). This serves as an ingredient of love. You cannot say you love and not care or be interested. Once your partner knows that you truly care, it is easy for communication lines to open.

- **Peaceful conversation**
  "But the wisdom that is from above is first pure, then peaceable, gentle, and easy to be intreated, full of mercy and good fruits, without partiality, and without hypocrisy". James 3:17 KJV
  You must strive to have peaceful conversations. If the conversation is getting heated up because of one party, it might just be better and easier to either wait or allow the upset party to cool down or postpone the conversation for another time.

    When a conversation is heated up, it can quickly turn into a shouting match and when two people are shouting, each individual will only be interested in who shouts louder and hurts the other the more. Reasoning at that stage will have taken flight and anger will be what is being communicated. The issues at hand will remain unresolved. Therefore, to create an environment for effective communication, whereby both parties have an understanding of each other's point of view, it must be peaceful.

    The trick is to ensure that you try to speak in a lower voice than the other party who is getting heated up. Any attempt to match your spouse word for word or tone for tone will most likely lead to disaster. For a fruitful conversation, it must be peaceful and as the above scripture indicates, we must ask for wisdom from above.

- **Speak one after another**
  "Two monologues do not make a dialogue." -Jeff Daly
  If for whatever reason, you are both speaking at the same time, then it is obvious no one is listening and nothing will be achieved. You must learn to speak one after the other and all it takes is for one party to resolve to wait until the other party finishes speaking. While speaking one after the other, you must also be careful not to talk at each other.